Lillian Stepney

The Carousel of Life

Dark Horse Studio
Waterbury, Connecticut

To order additional copies of this book, contact:
Xlibris
844-714-8691
www.Xlibris.com
Orders@Xlibris.com

ISBN: Softcover   978-1-4257-3047-5
               Hardcover   978-1-4257-5074-9
               EBook   978-1-6698-5944-4

Library of Congress Control Number: 2006907875

Print information available on the last page

Rev. date: 12/08/2022

Contents

Sunrise, sunset
Round and round
Good times, bad times
Up and down
Reaching for the brass ring
That carries hopes and dreams,
Enjoy life
Before the music ends.

1. The Maple Leaf and I

Watching the autumn leaves falling gently
On the quiet swimming hole
Drifting slowly, so slowly as if reluctant to go
Faster, yet faster, to be swept over the falls
In a golden cascade
Of bright autumn colors in their final display.

Then, I saw a tiny wayward maple leaf
Dressed in red and gold
Caught up in an eddy, fighting brave and bold,
Around and around it spun, not ready to go
Yet not wanting to stay,
To and fro
Rebellious, defying each rippling wave
Perhaps, dwelling on past glories,
The inevitable to delay.

Dreamily I watched, tears now filled my eyes
We have so much in common, this little leaf and I
As against the whims of man and nature
Valiantly had we fought,
Desperate in its futility, for the battle we had lost.
It was gone, the maple leaf in all its glorious perfection
Leaving the water calm and quiet,
To mirror my lonely reflection.

2. Summer Past

As I walk along the trails of gold,
The autumn colors so bright and bold,
With red, brown, gold, and rust
Wander down these trails I must.
Awed by colors of every hue,
I walk slowly, sad and blue,
Then I see a color quite out of place,
Its faded beauty almost lost, without a trace.
I bend to take a closer look
And uncover it from its shady nook.
A delicate pink rose turned its face
As if to speak with tranquil grace,
Remember me?
Remember, when these golden days have passed
I blossomed and bloomed but my time went fast.
Enjoy all seasons for they will not last.
The delicate petals fell among the golden leaves,
Covering the ground beneath the vibrant maple tree.
They seemed to say, this is the way
Of all life,
Enjoy today, enjoy today.

3. Enchanted Moment

Up before the sun on a warm sunny day
To climb into the wagon and then away
Down the lane at a brisk trot
Over the meadow and across the lot
To pick up the milk from the clear cold spring
Happily anticipating the joy each new day brings.

Beautiful birds singing their favorite songs,
Songs to herald the coming of this bright new dawn.
The merry melody of the brook on its way
Over glistening rocks in a glorious display
Of rainbow colors falling in shimmering cascades,
To lay in quiet pools like a tired child after play.
Deep purple violets around the spring did abound,
Laying a lush fragrant carpet over the ground.
Tiny dewdrops sparkling like jewels on every leaf
Appear as elfin bells there at our feet.
The heady scent of wild flowers filled the summer air,
Lacy woodland ferns swaying in rhythm, everywhere.
Spellbound, I stood transfixed
By the magical beauty there.

Then a gentle word was softly spoken
The spell was shattered, the magic broken.
The sun now rising in fiery acclaim
As we rode across the meadow and up the lane.
Dad in awed silence, sitting beside me, so quietly
I knew this vision was not a childish fantasy
But an enchanted moment we both had shared.
I remember always his whispered reverent prayer,
We thank you, Lord, for this heavenly garden
So rare.

4. Jack o' Dandy

My tiny crystal ornament hanging from the shade
Awakened me with the musical tune it played,
Swaying with each gentle breeze
that through the window came.
But, I felt no joy, only a dull and aching pain,
For I had no friends, no love, no happiness at all
Despondency hung over me like a deadly pall
So I closed my eyes, hoping to erase
The cruel reality – my life – a total waste.
A sunbeam like a beacon in a storm
Played about my eyes,
Forcing me to open them, open them up wide.
In wonder there I saw a light shimmering on my wall,
'Twas a jack o' dandy from my childhood I recalled.
With a myriad of rainbow colors,
It danced around the room,
Happily jumping up and down
to the tiny crystal's tune.
Fascinated, I watched the mystical array
Of iridescent colors in their glorious display.
As the sun grew dim, the jack o' dandy disappeared.
I felt there was a message here, a message very clear.
"His Light" forever shining, brightens each new day,
So you will not falter
as you travel down life's highway.

5. Safely Home

They found him, in the morning, lying in the street
Cold and stiff, yet he looked so peacefully asleep.
He was old and worn, and ragged were his clothes,
But his face shone with an inner glow,
Beautiful in repose.
The curious crowd sneered with their scornful gaze
Cursing, as they grumbled,
No great loss, take the bum away.
Oh! My pity for humanity
For they will never know
He was unique among them, flawless,
Pure as purest gold.
He gave up all his worldly goods
To help more needy souls.
He had ambitions in the past
And many human goals,
But abandoned them as a man
In his search for truth,
For he truly loved the one
Who had made the sacrifice
So that all mankind – good or evil –
May find eternal life.
An angel came for him,
One cold and lonely night,
To carry him to heaven
Up through the star-filled sky,
Where he would meet his Lord
And forever with Him abide.
He knelt before the King
Who sat upon his golden throne,
And knew that he'd been blessed,
For he was safely home.

6. Lavender and Lace

They say you look so pretty in your lavender and lace,
A very nice way of putting me in my place.
For I am old but I feel so young
Needless to say, I'm not expected to join in the fun.
As once in awhile they come by to say
While rearranging my cozy lap robe, are you okay?
Or perhaps if they remember, may we fix you a plate?
I reply, "thank you for asking, but I just ate"

I wonder why they cannot see the silent pleading
in my eyes,
Or the determination I exert so I will not cry,
As I sit alone here in complete and abject misery,
In my lavender and lace so prettily.
Can't they see the frustration and discontent?
I feel just like a useless ornament.

I was never meant to age with wisdom and grace,
For I need to feel the sun so warm upon my face,
The exhilaration of the wind whipping
Through my hair,
To enjoy the thrill of hearty laughter if I dared,
To experience the freedom of the open road,
Rebellious I discard my cozy lap robe.

With the sun warm upon my face,
The wind whipping through my hair,
I call a "goodbye" to my shocked family standing there.
I loved your pretty lavender and lace,
So save them for me, please – for a much later date.

7. Love Birds

I looked out the window and what did I see?
A pretty little bird, looking back at me.
I coaxed him closer with crumbs of bread
Perhaps to stroke his soft feathered head.
Twisting and turning he studied me, up and down,
Eyes filling with fear, growing big and round.
Frightened, he flew to safety in a nearby tree,
Where precariously he perched, warily watching me.

I looked out the window and what did I see?
Two pretty love birds, looking back at me.
One was bright, one was not, truly a Jack and Jill,
Enjoying the treat on my window sill.
Showing no fear as they enjoyed this treat,
Before flying off to their special retreat.
Close to a cozy nest, snuggled in the nearby tree,
Sitting contently, cuddling, ignoring me.

I looked out the window and what did I see?
Six pretty little birds, looking back at me.
Jack was singing, so was Jill,
Wanting to share their joy with me,
Before flying off to their family tree.
Awakened by twittering, chirping, whirring of wings,
A real cacophony of familiar noises and things.

I looked out the window and what did I see?
Four love birds building nests in the nearby tree.
Working frantically, what a ruckus they made,
Happily anticipating this homecoming day.
Diligently, twig by twig and straw by straw,
Laboring to finish this much-needed chore
As tiny nests were snuggled, safe and secure.
They hovered above them, making doubly sure,
Before flying off to the window sill,
Hoping a few crumbs would be there still.

I looked out the window and what did I see?
Ten little birds looking back at me.
'Twas getting crowded on that window sill,
There was no room for my pretty Jack and Jill.
Babies, pushing and shoving, to get their fair share
Of the crumbs so generously sprinkled there.
Jack and Jill sadly looking back at me,
Before flying off to safety in the nearby tree.

8. It Only Takes One to Lead

Lingering in the park one day
Enjoying the antics of the people as they played,
Suddenly a voice rang out with an urgent warning
You all must leave, for a violent storm is coming.
In panic, the people started a mad dash towards home,
But abruptly stopped – stunned – by a young soldier
Standing alone.
His proud gaze turned upward,
Watching our colors flying high,
Whipping and snapping, frantically yet bravely,
In the stormy sky.
He did not look special or in any way unique,
Until the awed and quiet crowd listened to him speak.
Was he whispering a solemn prayer?
Or a plea for help in making them aware?
Tentatively, one by one, then swiftly in unison,
Young and old,
Came to stand with him – there – around the flagpole.
With passion he said, "We must lower
Our stars and stripes,
To keep it safe throughout this day
And through the coming night."

Even the howling wind had stilled
As they lowered our flag down,
Silently, so silently, fold by fold, it must not touch
The ground,
Heedless to the fury of the storm
For they had lost their fear.
Then the awesome silence broke
Into a rousing cheer.
They had battled the elements, the stars and stripes
They had saved,
As reverently, so reverently,
Tucked Old Glory safely away.

9. Cage of Love

In years I am old, I must admit
But still I am blessed with all my wits.
I'm the same person of so many years ago,
Will always love skating and sledding in the snow,
To feel the exhilaration as the wind whips
Through my hair,
Enjoying the fun most anywhere.
A good fast swim in summer's heat
Racing with the little ones, they are sure to beat.
Hiking the trails in the golden days of fall,
Raking and piling high the pretty leaves,
Romping in them all.
So, I sit in boredom with my memories
For the tender loving care has made a prisoner of me.
I'll break these silken and velvet walls, you will agree,
When you see me laughing
As I burn the old rocking chair
In anticipation for a good old time at the county fair.

10. Rose of Sharon

The sweet scent of hyacinth,
Beauty of the sunny daffodil,
Purity of the lily
And the golden jonquil,
Paled and were lost,
Gaudy in their dazzling display,
As a dainty, delicate "Rose"
Was born to us that day.
Cute and cuddly, she was tiny,
Dimpled, pink and warm,
As tenderly as daddy
Gently placed her into my waiting arms.
Her hair, a flaxen halo shining
Like a golden crown,
Innocent eyes looking into mine,
Soft and velvety brown.
Rosebud mouth pursed,
As if awaiting her first kiss,
Our wee fragile flower, our darling little miss.
A potpourri of love and joy,
hope and fear combined,
but love triumphed over all
as our hearts entwined.
A perfect "Rose", a rose without thorns,
Our lovely Rose of Sharon
To us that day was born.

11. Memories

The door flew open and she stood there
In the cold and frosty air
Breathless, a picture so fresh and fair
A moment in time so very rare.
Hair soft as shimmering gold
Made brighter still by the wintry cold,
Eyes of green with excitement dancing,
Straight and tall like a young colt prancing.
Her rosy lips smiling, she said,
"Grandma, come!"
Holding hands we rushed outside – what fun!
A glistening snowman caught my eye
A little bit lopsided, a little bit awry,
Sparkling there in the cold winter air.
This, with me, she just had to share.
I handed her a hat and scarf
To finish off her work of art.
Her questing eyes sought mine, seeking
To read my thoughts without speaking.
Did I think of her as clever?
Did I appreciate her endeavor?
I wonder if she will ever know
I hardly saw that man of snow
For the image of His perfection dancing there
Left a precious memory, forever shared.

12. Precious Gifts

Two little rascals splashing in the brook
Fishing for pollywogs without benefit of hook.

Two little rascals holding skirts up high
Pretending yes, pretending to stay dry.

Two little rascals soon soaking wet
Oh, what would they do, would you like to make a bet?

Two little rascals had heard tales of old
Catch a magic penny bug and put it in your shoe.

Two little rascals believed what they were told
Penny bugs turn to bright and shiny pennies
Just for you.

Two little rascals were quick to decide
We can catch so many penny bugs, if we really try.

Two little rascals in mutual consent
Ran through the garden, dripping as they went.

Two little rascals filled with childish pride
So sure that mom would be happy
When given her surprise.

Two little rascals suddenly ill at ease
Mom was not smiling, she seemed very displeased.

Two little rascals hurriedly explained,
"We caught them just for you",
As they offered the penny bugs
Trapped in their shoes.

Two little rascals standing there wet and cold,
She took them in her arms to caress and to hold.

Two little rascals, she murmured,
"You are my precious gifts",
As she placed upon each one
A mother's tender kiss.

13. Stepping Stones

Upon this gently sloping hill
There is a garden where
Beneath the fallen blossoms fair
My love lies sleeping there...
My wild, wild Bill.
In memory of my love.

Dolly

14. Rendezvous

In the awesome still of the early spring morn',
A small figure sat on an old stone wall,
Face upturned, waiting for the coming dawn.
A hush held all creatures silent, both large and small.
A blanket of peace tangible, with love so deep,
A picture of beauty, complete and serene,
God must have enveloped all in His arms to keep
This one heavenly place for her, it would seem.
The essence of His presence
Sitting beside her there,
Opened her heart – her soul lay bare.

The sudden song of the woodland thrush,
A stirring rustling in the brush,
The wondrous spell was broken, no longer alone,
The small figure jumped from the wall
And walked the path to home.
Bursting through the kitchen door
To tell the wonder of it all,
No words would come, like a hand was gently laid
Across her lips, as if to say,
"Those moments were special for me and for you,
Keep them sacred, until our rendezvous."

Many years have passed with strife and struggle,
Many hopes shattered like wind-swept bubbles.
Now the frail figure sits and waits
Silent, dreaming as she meditates,
Perhaps she dreams of wildflowers in the spring
Or an old stone wall
Where the Lord looks over all.
She sits alone and waits for you,
To keep that secret rendezvous.

15. A Promise Kept

Forlornly the frail girl sat on the littered walk
Leaning weakly against the dirty graffito wall,
Watching the hurrying people rushing by
Contempt showing clearly in their eyes,
They did not know nor did they care
About the frail girl weeping there.

Bowing her head in deep despair
With trembling lips whispered a prayer,
"Oh, Lord," she cried, "I am lost and so alone,
I promise Lord, I will atone
For all my sinful wasted years
That caused so many bitter tears.
Oh, Lord, take me from this living hell,
Save me, Lord, if it be thy will."

Then, in the rustling of the leaves,
A voice softly as a summer breeze
Whispered gently, "Have no fear,
I am with you now."
A hand soft and cool touched
Her fevered brow.
I have heard your promise and your prayer,
For I am with you everywhere,
You were never abandoned, lost, or alone,
He scolded in His firm but tender tone,
I also made a promise that I must keep,
All you had to do was open your heart and speak.
With a contented sigh,
She drifted off to sleep.

16. The Valley

Drifting slowly down
Into a valley misty and gray
With twisting, shifting shadows,
Lost souls gone astray.
Billowing rolling clouds
Like mighty ocean swells,
Swirling mists embracing her
As they rose and fell,
Captured in this seething tide
But still unafraid,
For she was not alone
As she rode this turbulent wave.

Carried by His radiant light,
Safely to a pristine shore,
Where an angel fair stood,
Guarding a massive door.
Timidly she approached
As she heard the angel speak,
"You have made a promise,
A promise you must keep."
The angel turned and pointed,
The door swung open wide,
He bade her enter
As he firmly guided her inside.

17. Eden

Transfixed by the vision she beheld
'Twas a heavenly place where only angels dwell.
As in a dream she walked,
Urged on by an unseen hand,
Through a garden paradise created by
Our Master's plan.
Following a path of shimmering gold
Laced with precious gems,
Such peace and tranquility
Never known by earthly man.
This golden path led to
A quiet shady nook,
With crystal water tumbling musically
Into a laughing brook,
Where contentedly an angel sat
Smiling as she passed,
Petting a lion at his knee,
A lamb upon his lap.
The sparkling golden path
Faded fast away,
Turning to retrace her steps,
She had lost her way.
'Twas then she saw the tiny sign
Pointing to the rainbow's end,
A small, brown path
Just around the bend.

18. Rainbow's End

Struggling through the thicket,
Was it all in vain?
Then she sensed an inner voice
Reminding her once again,
That she had made a promise,
A promise that she must keep.
Weary and exhausted, she fell into
A deep and troubled sleep.
Awakening refreshed,
Breathless at the splendor of the scene,
There was a meadow of wildflowers
Fragrant, pure and clean,
A rainbow of delicate pastels
Declaring His promise made of old,
Embracing a glorious sunrise
Just starting to unfold.
There was a golden chariot,
The door stood open wide,
Where two winged snow-white horses
Pranced about with pride.
They seemed to be waiting
As she timidly approached,
But as she neared, the door swung shut
Upon the golden coach.
Then a voice firmly stated
From somewhere deep within,
"You have made a promise you must keep
Before you're free of sin."
On command, the snow-white horses flew up
The rainbow, the stairway to the sky,
Up towards the starry universe
To vanish in the heavens high.

19. Going Home

The girl no longer frail
Stood up straight and tall,
Pushing away from
The dirty graffito wall,
With her dreams
Still burning brightly in her eyes,
Watching closely
The rushing people as they hurried by,
Surprised by smiles instead of scorn
When they glanced her way,
Children no longer avoiding her,
More inclined to play.
The inner voice guiding her
Freed her from all fear,
Remembering her dreams
Knowing He was always near.
With renewed hope and confidence,
She boarded the bus to home,
Vowing to keep her covenant
When she promised to atone.

20. His Message

The whispering of angel voices
Soft as a summer breeze,
Murmuring so gently,
Do not sorrow, do not grieve.
Your love sends a message,
A message you must hear,
So fill your heart with gladness,
Wipe away your tears.
Feel his joy as you listen – while he sings,
For he is happy among us
In the shelter of our wings.

21. I Believe

I sit among the roses
Upon a marble bench
Dreaming of fun and laughter
That so quickly came and went.
Silently here I sit
As I quietly reminisce.
I feel his arms about me
And his sweet and tender kiss.
I see the twinkle in his eyes
As he gazes into mine
We were young and happy
'Twas another place in time.
Lovingly I planted
A garden we will share
A garden of memories
With flowers bright and fair.
I know his earthly body
Will slowly turn to dust
But our Lord has made a promise
In this I place my trust.
There will be no tears of sorrow
Or suffering earthly pain,
For as He promised,
My love is whole again.
His spirit free and soaring
Far above the cloudy sky,
To meet a heavenly host
Waiting there in the heavens high
Where he has joined the angels
In watching over us.
Our Lord's promise now fulfilled
Believe in this I must.

22. The Garden

In the beauty of this garden
  Angels linger near

Where the sweet scent of blossoms
  Drift softly upon the air

Bringing memories of my love
  Sleeping so peacefully there

I know he is with Father
  In His eternal tender care

My heart fills with gladness
  As I wipe away my tears.

23. Peace

I stand beside this tiny plot,
   My love lies beneath.
He feels no pain or sorrow
   Nor endless human grief,
For his tired body rests
   In deep and tranquil sleep,
His spirit free from earthly woes.

24. Carousel of Life

The sun rises, the sun sets
   As the earth revolves round and round,
Like crashing cymbals, the high tide crests
   To flow back gently for a needed rest.
Riding high or riding low, a constant up and down,
   Always trying to catch the elusive brass ring,
Forever seeking to achieve your hopes and dreams.
   The sun will rise, the sun will set,
   The cycle begins again,
Like a giant carousel, up and down, round and round,
   As life goes on and on, till the music ends.

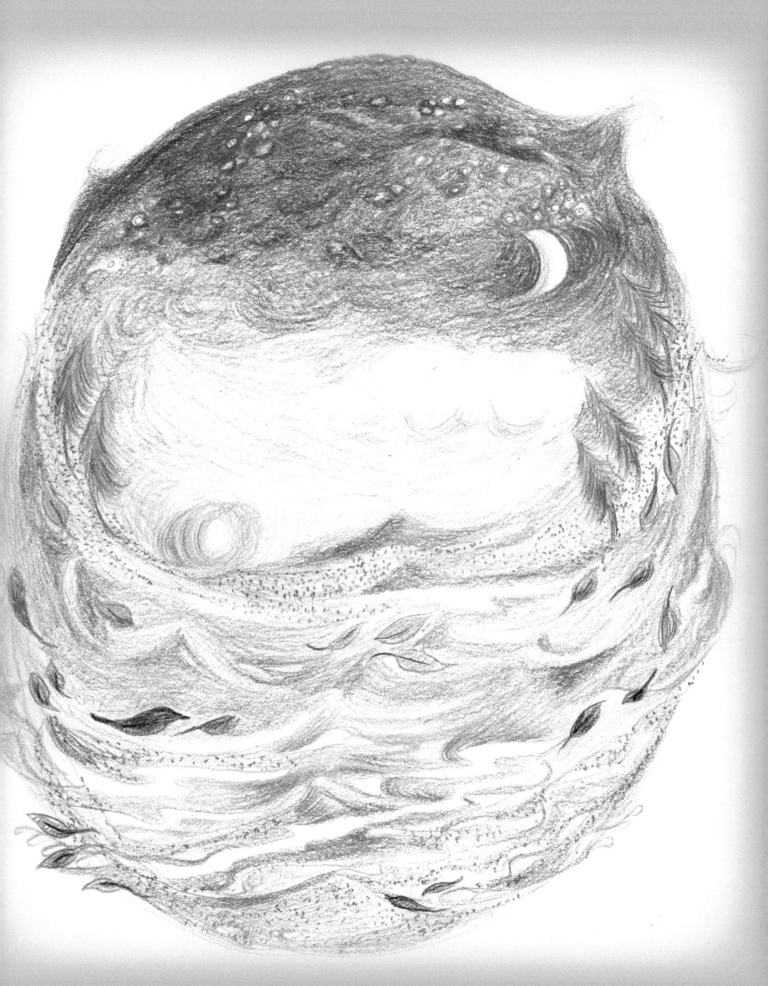

Lillian Geneveive Stepney

Born Lillian Sears, March 6, 1917.

Lillian spent her childhood on her family's small fruit and dairy farm on a high plateau overlooking a city in beautiful New England. This setting seemed magical in its simplistic beauty. As a child, she enjoyed the love of parents and grandparents and a superbly happy childhood.

As Lillian grew older, she walked many miles through wilderness areas with only her thoughts for company. She excelled at skating and swimming, for she loved the rigors of the great outdoors. Evenings would find her cuddled behind her grandma's large ornate stove, content with a piece of fruit, pad and pencil, creating a poem or short story.

Life changed dramatically with the onslaught of the Great Depression. Her family life suffered deeply, bringing on illness, tragedies, and complete economic collapse. These hard times brought about a new aspect to her consciousness. These memories are reflected in her poetry, with just a hint of the mystical as she recalls the happier times of her earlier childhood.

Her leisure time is now spent gardening as she conjures up another poem reflecting upon the life and times of long ago, both tragic and mystical as she recaptures the days long flown.

Her mother called her Lillian, after her favorite flower. Her father, a farmer familiar with plant terminology, called her PIPS – the tiny seed that creates all life to the Lily family.

Thus, in memory of her Pa Pa, she chooses PIPS as her pen name.

Christmas 2005

Printed in the United States
by Baker & Taylor Publisher Services